T0024373

fish farts

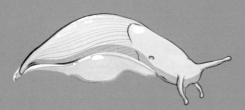

To Mika and Brady, who make everything worthwhile

ATHENEUM BOOKS FOR YOUNG READERS • An imprint of Simon & Schuster Children's Publishing Division • 1230 Avenue of the Americas, New York, New York 10020 • Text © 2024 by Joanne Settel • Illustration © 2024 by Natasha Donovan • Book design © 2024 by Simon & Schuster, LLC • All rights reserved, including the right of reproduction in whole or in part in any form. • ATHENEUM BOOKS FOR YOUNG READERS is a registered trademark of Simon & Schuster, LLC. Atheneum logo is a trademark of Simon & Schuster, LLC. • Simon & Schuster: Celebrating 100 Years of Publishing in 2024 • For information about special discounts for bulk purchases, please contact Simon & Schuster Special Sales at 1-866-506-1949 or business@simonandschuster.com. • The Simon & Schuster Speakers Bureau can bring authors to your live event. For more information or to book an event, contact the Simon & Schuster Speakers Bureau at 1-866-248-3049 or visit our website at www.simonspeakers.com. • The text for this book was set in Joanna MT Std. • The illustrations for this book were rendered digitally. • Manufactured in China • 0324 SCP • First Edition • 10 9 8 7 6 5 4 3 2 1 • Library of Congress Cataloging-in-Publication Data • Names: Settel, Joanne, author. | Donovan, Natasha, illustrator. • Title: Fish farts : and other amazing ways animals adapt / Joanne Settel ; illustrated by Natasha Donovan. • Description: New York : Atheneum Books for Young Readers, [2024] | Includes bibliographical references. | Audience: Ages 4-8 | Audience: Grades 2-3 | Summary: "Pop off a tail, roll around in dung, or simply fart to send a message! These are just a few of the many astounding ways that animals have adapted to their environments. Animals trick, trap, or fry predators; they feed on other animals' poop and skin; they use electric zaps, slime, and other unexpected methods to communicate. Featuring animals like Komodo dragon lizards, bombardier beetles, and capuchin monkeys, read about the surprising, exciting, and sometimes hilarious ways that animals survive and thrive"— Provided by publisher. • Identifiers: LCCN 2023026782 (print) | LCCN 2023026783 (ebook) | ISBN 9781665918831 (hardcover) | ISBN 9781665918848 (ebook) • Subjects: LCSH: Animals—Adaptation—Juvenile literature. | Animal defenses—Juvenile literature. • Classification: LCC QH546 .S47 2024 (print) | LCC QH546 (ebook) | DDC 578.4—dc23/eng/20231109 • LC record available at https://lccn.loc.gov/2023026782 • LC ebook record available at https://lccn.loc.gov/2023026783

fish farts

And Other Amazing Ways Animals Adapt

Joanne Settel, PhD

Illustrated by Natasha Donovan

Atheneum Books for Young Readers

NEW YORK LONDON TORONTO SYDNEY NEW DELHI

Green Blood—page 31

STICKY, STINKY, SLIMY ANIMAL TRICKS, TRAPS, AND MORE

Pop off a tail, roll around in dung, fly into a hummingbird's nose—these are just a few of the many amazing, astounding ways that animals have adapted to their environments. They trick, trap, or fry predators; they feed on other animals' poop and skin; they use farts, slime, or other unexpected methods to communicate. Read on to learn about the surprising, exciting, and sometimes hilarious ways that animals survive and thrive.

speaking with slime

When a slug wants to chase away a rival, it does so with a smear of **slime**. These shell-less snails are covered in a slippery coat that carries its own special scent. That smelly slime allows slugs to sense if another slug is nearby, and whether it's a mate or a challenger.

Every time a slug leaves its burrow, it creates a stream of gooey slime, helping the slug glide safely over sharp rocks and twigs, and leaving behind a smelly, sticky trail. That means a slug can follow the scent of its own trail to find its way back home, or avoid the path of another slug. If it makes a mistake, though, it can end up attacked in a rival's burrow.

Slugs also make another kind of slime: one containing chemicals called **pheromones** that act as mating calls. This slime sends the message "I'm ready" to other slugs.

Slugs also need their coat of slime to stay alive. These soft-bodied animals are usually protected from water loss inside their moist burrows. Outside, though, a slimeless slug risks losing so much water, it might turn into a dried-out splat. Luckily, when they're outside munching on leaves, worms, **feces**, and other yummy slug food, their protective slime coats keep them from drying out.

Sticky slime even helps slugs cling as they climb up trees and glide on the undersides of twigs. Clearly, slime is an all-purpose solution!

1. Slug slime may seem super gross, but humans make lots of similar slimy mucus. Both slime and mucus are a sticky, slippery mix of **sugar** and **protein** molecules. Like slug slime, our mucus has lots of critical functions that help keep us alive. In the nose and the breathing tubes—or **respiratory tract**—a **mucus lining** traps any dirt we breathe in and helps fight invading **microbes**. In the **digestive tract**, mucus smooths the movement of passing food, protecting the walls of the stomach from damaging chemicals.

2. Slimy salamanders make a slime so sticky that it can glue the mouth of a **predatory** garter snake shut. Unable to close its jaws, the snake waves its head around, trying to remove the glue. Meanwhile, the speckled salamander has time to escape from the snake's mouth. If you tried to pick up one of these **amphibians**, its slime would cement your fingers together and be almost impossible to remove!

fish farts

How do a million herring fish swim together at night without smacking into one another? They use a stream of **farts**! A herring can shoot out forty farts in one second! That's a lot of gas, and it turns out to be a great way to communicate.

Like human farts, herring farts are bubbles of gas that pop out of the **anus**. But unlike human farts, herring farts don't come from **digested** food, and they're never stinky. Fish farts come from air that the fish gulps when it comes to the surface of the water. The air gets swallowed into a sack called the **swim bladder**. A swim bladder's main job is to move a fish up and down in the water by filling and emptying with gas. "Fart talk" is a way to get more use out of something herring already do.

Farts are a great way to send messages in the dark. Since herring have excellent hearing, each fish can tell from the fart pops just how close its neighbors are and maintain a steady distance from them. This is how hundreds of thousands of herring form a **school**, swimming together for hours in perfect, neat lines. These schools only work if the fish can **synchronize**, working together to space themselves properly. Clouds of fart bubbles turn out to be a great way to do just that.

Herring form their giant schools because there's safety in numbers. At around one foot in length, a herring can easily get snatched up by a hungry whale, seal, shark, or bird. By staying in a pack, most of the herring are hidden. So even if a predatory shark gets close enough to snap up a mouthful from the outer parts of the school, the rest of the fish remain well protected in the middle.

But if the herring can hear these farts, why can't the predators? It turns out the high-pitched, squeaky farts can't be heard by most fish-eating creatures. Whales and dolphins can hear those pitches, so the sounds do attract those predators. Still, staying in a school of farters is worth the risk.

1. Killer farts! The beaded lacewing is a long-winged insect that kills its termite prey with poisonous farts. Female lacewings lay their eggs in a termite-filled log. Once the eggs hatch, the tiny wormlike **larvae** fart a poison gas to stun the much bigger termite. A quick spray of the toxic brew makes the termites stop moving. Then, the hungry larvae chomp down on their motionless prey.

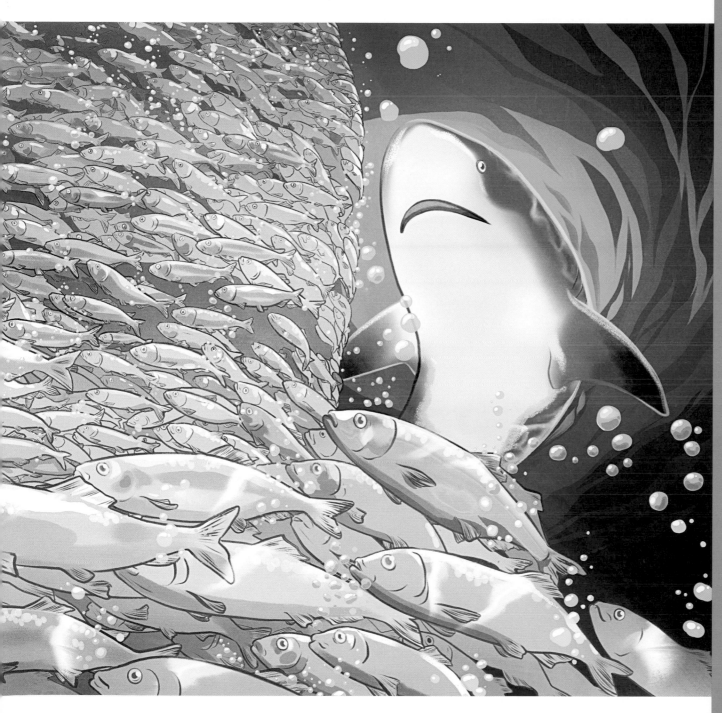

**2. Do all animals fart?
Many do.** Mammals like elephants, giraffes, dogs, cats, orangutans, and dolphins fart. So do reptiles and amphibians like frogs and snakes, and insects like cockroaches. With so many farters out there, it may surprise you to learn that scientists have not been able to observe farting birds! With their short digestive tracts, birds don't build up gas in their intestines, so these feathered fliers seem to be fart-proof.

3. Termites are super farters. These wood-eating insects release enough stinky methane gas to contribute to the greenhouse effect and increase global warming. Luckily, some of this methane is absorbed by bacteria living in the termite mounds, so these insects aren't the worst offenders. The real air polluters are cows, who release thirty to fifty gallons of methane a day. Surprisingly, most cow gas comes from burps, while only about 5 percent is from farts and manure.

a shocking tail

A zap of electricity is a strange way to attract a mate! For electric elephantnose fish, though, it's a perfect way to communicate. These slightly electric African fish with a long upper lip (not a nose, as the name wrongly suggests) send out **electric pulses** for everything from finding their way through a cloudy stream to chasing off rivals. So, using these pulses to also attract mates makes a lot of sense. Luckily, elephantnoses only send out weak pulses, so they don't hurt one another with their zaps.

Humans also have an electric charge! More specifically, our muscles constantly fire electric pulses. We can use special medical devices to pick up the electricity from our skin, but the pulse is too weak to sense on our own. We also can't control how the electricity gets directed. Electric fish do both. They create their "shocking talk" with **electric organs** in their tails. These superfast organs send out over eighty pulses in one second—just the blink of an eye. They send different messages by changing the **frequencies** (speeds) of the pulses. Messages can communicate "I'm ready to mate" or "Get out of my territory."

Along with sending signals, these amazing fish can sense incoming messages using small **electroreceptors**—or electricity sensors—scattered over their heads, backs, and bellies. While humans can only sense a strong or weak electric shock, electric fish understand all kinds of different "pulse talk" with their highly sensitive receptors.

Elephantnoses are just one of over four hundred **species** of weakly electric fish. They live in cloudy rivers and streams in Africa and South America and are active at night. In a habitat where it's almost impossible to see a thing, "electric talk" is a wonderful way to figure out who is friend or foe.

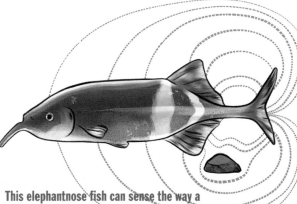

This elephantnose fish can sense the way a rock changes the shape of its electric field.

1. Weakly electric fish don't just "talk" electrically—they also "see" with electricity. When an electric fish sends out pulses, it forms a **dipole field**, or circle of electricity, that surrounds the fish's body. Whenever the fish swims past an object, the shape of its field changes. This fish can sense this change and guess at the size and shape of the object it is passing.

2. Sharks are electricity super sensors. They don't "talk" electrically, but they can pick up very tiny charges coming from their prey. Like humans, all other living animals have a small electric charge that comes from their working muscles. The electroreceptors scattered over a shark's head are so sensitive that they can even pick up charges from a fish buried in the sandy bottom of the ocean. Sharks begin searching for prey by smell, but once a victim is a few feet away, it's electricity that allows sharks to precisely locate and snatch their meal from its hiding place.

what an elephant knows through its sensitive toes

There's danger nearby! Elephants have spotted a lion. The giant mammals rumble and roar and stomp their feet. Two miles away, a lone bull elephant feeding on leaves senses the warning—not with his ears but with his toes! The sounds are too far away to reach him through the air, but the **vibrations** in the ground travel for miles and miles. You can feel vibrations in the floor when someone plays very loud music or if you put your hand over your closed mouth and hum.

The bull elephant tunes right in when he feels the ground rumble. He presses his toes to the ground as the vibrations spread up his toes and around his body. They travel through his leg bones all the way up to his **ossicles**, which are tiny bones deep inside his ears. The elephant feels the message and knows just what this kind of vibration means: a **predator** is nearby, and it's time to move on.

Ground vibrations communicate many different messages, and elephants can tell one kind of vibration from another, whether it's a warning of danger or a call for a mate.

It's not easy for a male elephant to find a mate. Adult males, or **bulls**, live alone, far from herds of females and young. To make things even trickier, elephant females, or cows, are only in **estrous** (ready to mate) for just a few days every four or five years. So, bulls need to get the timing just right. Vibrations are a great way to do this. Cows send out a powerful call, and the bulls who are in **musth** and ready for a mate send out their own pulsing rumbles, working together to pick up these sounds and find one another.

Young elephants also use rumbles to call to the herd when they are lost, and bulls defend their territories from other males with rumbles and roars. There are many kinds of vibrations to sort through, but somehow, the elephants do it all with their sensitive toes.

1. A termite hitting its head on the ground isn't much of an alarm, right? Well, we might not be able to sense it, but fellow termites will. So when an African termite soldier drums its head on the ground to warn its colony that a termite-eating aardvark is near, other termites take off. At eleven beats per second, the drumming creates vibrations over a foot away. As the vibrations move through termite nest passageways, other soldiers pick up the beat and pass it on. That's enough to get the message through a thirty-foot-high nest, allowing thousands of termites to flee to safety.

2. The female fringed jumping spider, an Australian spider-eating spider, is the master of trickery. It creates vibrations to trap other species of jumping spiders and turn them into a meal. Spiders use their legs to sense the vibrations of prey stuck in their webs or to detect mating vibrations from other spiders. Fringed spiders take advantage of this special sense, drawing other spiders right into their waiting fangs.

3. One spider that's easy to trick is the Bleeker's jumping spider. A hungry fringed spider shakes a Bleeker's leaf nest, just like a male Bleeker would. When the female comes out looking for a mate, she finds a fringed spider instead. The trickster jabs the Bleeker with its venomous fangs, paralyzing and feasting on its eight-legged victim.

nose-picking pals

You can pick your friend, you can pick your nose, but you can't pick your friend's nose, unless you are a capuchin monkey. These long-tailed primates have an unusual way of making friends. They stick their fingers up onc another's noses! When they're feeling extra friendly, they may also poke a finger into their buddy's eye socket and squeeze. You'd think annoyed monkeys would run from their picking, poking pals, but they don't seem to mind at all. They may even get things going by grabbing another monkey's finger to put into their own nostril. This weird behavior can go on for as long as an hour with both monkeys poking and swaying. Even if one monkey sneezes, the game doesn't stop. The other monkey just pulls out its finger and puts it back in again.

Nose picking and eye poking are ways that capuchins bond with one another. These small, six-to-nine-pound South and Central American tree monkeys spend much of their days in packs of ten or more, leaping through the trees and hunting for insects, fruit, leaves, birds, and frogs to eat. Sticking together is a great way to stay safe. When one monkey

1. Capuchins have other strange ways of bonding beyond nose picking. They suck one another's tails and ears, sit on one another's heads, and—perhaps oddest of all—they sometimes bite a clump of hair off a friend's face and hold it in their teeth. Then the two monkeys pass the clump of fur back and forth between them. Ouch!

2. Sometimes, capuchins pee on their hands and rub the liquid on their feet. This "urine washing" behavior seems odd, but when urine dries, it's sticky. Scientists think that urine-covered, sticky hands and feet help capuchins get a better grip as they climb from branch to branch. Who would think a little pee would get you up a tree?

spots a predator like a coyote, snake, or eagle, it calls in alarm so the group can chase off the predator or dash into the trees.

Since being part of a group is so important, capuchins spend lots of time together touching, sniffing, and grooming, picking dirt and insects off one another's fur. Lots of different monkeys and apes connect with their packmates or form bonds through close contact. But nose picking and eye poking—now those are capuchin specialties!

don't eat me, i'm dung!

Wearing a stinky coat of pig poop? Yuck! But for young Komodo dragon lizards, it's a lifesaver. At eight or more feet long, adult Komodos are the largest lizards in the world. The giant predators fill their bellies with anything they can catch, including birds, lizards, rabbits, pigs, deer, and even other Komodos. But the stink of poop can be a great defense.

Komodos depend on smell when they hunt. Using long, forked yellow tongues, the lizards catch the scent particles of their prey in the air. Once they sense a future meal, the giant lizards dash out, knock it over, and sink their large, curved teeth into the hide. Komodos eat quickly, wasting almost nothing. Muscle, bone, hooves, belly, and skin all go down the hatch. But there is one thing Komodos stay far away from: poop (scientifically called feces or **dung**). When they get to a prey's poop-filled intestines, the giant lizards swing the guts around and around. The poop goes flying, and the Komodo gobbles down the rest of their meal.

That means poop can protect young Komodos. From the moment they hatch out of their eggs, the juvenile lizards are in danger of being eaten. At a bit more than one foot long, a newborn Komodo is already big for a lizard, but compared to an eight-foot adult, it's small. Small enough to eat. So, a young lizard stays up in the trees for around two years, avoiding their larger counterparts.

Once it's around four feet in length, the growing Komodo heads down to the ground to hunt larger prey. Though bigger, these two-year-old lizards are still in danger. So, to stay protected, the youngsters turn themselves into a poop-covered Komodo roll. They may not smell wonderful, but they'll live to see another day!

1. Komodo dragons aren't the only animals that coat themselves in dung. Giant pandas do it too! These large black-and-white mammals smear themselves with fresh horse manure until their fur is completely covered. Pandas seem to do this only when it is cold outside, so scientists suspect the manure is a rather gross, extra warm winter coat.

2. Smearing on a layer of dung is one thing, but some animals make a home of it! Tiny narrow-mouthed frogs living in Sri Lanka spend their summer days buried inside chunks of Asian elephant dung. The damp droppings protect the one-inch frogs from drying out. And since the waste is also home to beetles, ants, crickets, and other insects, it provides lots of yummy food for the frogs as well.

whale poop for lunch

Whale poop for lunch? Add bits of whale skin and whale lice (tiny shrimplike **parasites**), and you've got a yummy meal for a whale sucker! Also known as a remora, this long, skinny fish spends its life riding on the back or belly of a whale, picking up plenty of food along the way.

To stay on a whale while it's traveling up to twenty-five miles an hour, a remora needs a way to hang on very, very tightly. The clingy fish does this with its own built-in **suction cup**, a large flat disk on the top of its head. The disk, which looks a lot like the bottom of a sneaker, has rows of small, thin **barbed** bones called **lamella** all surrounded by a thick suction lip. Since the disc sits on the top of its head, the remora actually rides its **host** upside down.

Not only does the remora easily cling to its live blubber boat, it also easily unhooks. When this whale rider wants to eat, it pops off and gobbles up anything on, over, and under its host. And if it's looking for a mate, no problem! There are usually ten or more other remoras hanging on right nearby to choose from. What a life!!!

You might think that a whale would get annoyed by the slimy passengers clinging to its sides, but the carrier gets something out of the deal. Remoras gobble up nasty lice that dig into the whale's skin and mouth to dine on its flesh. When both animals benefit from a relationship, it's called **mutualism**, which is a type of **symbiosis**. It's a good deal for everyone: the whale gets cleaned of parasites, and the remora gets mouthfuls of delicious little critters and whale poop.

A remora fish showing the large suction cup on the top of its head.

1. Whales are just one of the many hosts that whale suckers use to hitch a ride. These fish are also found clinging to dolphins and can hang on even when a dolphin leaps from the water. There are seven other species of remoras who glom onto sharks, skates, turtles, and big fish. Some even attach themselves to ships and divers, though they're not likely to get much food on those rides.

2. When a small wrasse fish swims into the mouth of a predator, it's not trying to get eaten; it's trying to eat! Like the remora, the wrasse goes after parasites that **infect** bigger fish. A four-inch

wrasse can poke right into a predator's mouth and gills without getting swallowed. That's because the predatory host fish stays very still, allowing the wrasse to clean it as part of a mutualistic relationship. In fact, cod, eels, sharks, and other large predators actually seek out the cleaners. With their bright blue-and-yellow coloring, cleaner wrasse stand out so their hosts can easily find them. A single wrasse can service two thousand big fish in one day!

3. It's not just fish that provide cleaning services. Imagine hitching a ride on the back of a dangerous rhinoceros— that's what oxpecker birds do! These red-beaked birds eat ticks off the backs of rhinos and other hosts like zebras and giraffes. This is partly good for the host mammals, but oxpeckers have a sneaky little trick. While they are picking off a tick, the birds often dig a little deeper, sucking up some of the host's blood and leaving little sores behind. So, while the relationship is mutualistic, it's also parasitic, making it a win for the oxpecker, but only a partial success for the rhino.

sloth poop and moth eggs—a perfect pair

Sloth moths have very unusual requirements for their offspring: they will only lay their eggs in sloth poop. But sloth poop's not easy to find! Three-toed sloths only **defecate** or poop once a week, so the moths have to be patient. Luckily, these insects live in the sloth's fur, ready and waiting for the big event. When it's finally time, the sloth climbs down from its tree, digs a hole in the ground, and defecates. Then, female moths fly from their furry homes and lay their eggs in the poop.

Newly hatched moth larvae feed on the poop (or feces) until they **metamorphose** from caterpillars into winged adult moths. Then, they fly off in search of a new sloth to live on. They often join over one hundred other moths scattered all over the sloth's fur. The sloth moths mate and feed on the smelly, green **algae** that grow all over a sloth. They also use their long, sucking mouthparts, or **proboscises**, to suck juices from the sloth's skin and eyeballs. It's a perfect all-purpose home for the moth.

But what about the sloth? You'd think that a sloth would want to get rid of the pesky tenants, but it turns out that the sloth may get something out of the deal. When the moths die, they leave behind **nutrients** that help the green fur algae grow. And a healthy algae coat can be a lifesaver. Sloths are very, very slow-moving mammals that spend nearly all their time hanging upside down from a tree branch munching on nearby leaves. The green algae **camouflage** the sloths, making them look like the leafy green branches they hang from. This, along with their extra-slow movement, makes sloths very hard for predators to spot. Algae also are sloth food, adding extra nutrition to their leafy diet. A little poop for the moths and an algae coat for the sloth turn into a perfect combination.

The sloth comes down from the tree to poop, while the moths fly off the sloth to lay their eggs in the droppings.

1. Sloths do everything upside down! They eat, sleep, mate, and even give birth hanging by their long, curved claws. These claws are attached to special **tendons** that lock in place around a tree limb, allowing these super-slow mammals to hang for hours without much effort. A sloth's liver, stomach, and other organs are attached to the ribs and hips, which hold everything in place to avoid squishing the sloth's lungs.

2. When a sloth leaves a tree to poop, it's a big, big deal. Since it only does this once a week, it lets go of a lot of poop all at once—as much as three to five pounds of waste! A three-toed sloth can shrink from nine to six pounds with a single poop. But this process can be pretty risky. When they're on the ground, sloths risk being eaten by predators like eagles, jaguars, and ocelots. So, why go to all the trouble? Scientists don't know for sure, but they're investigating those giant piles of sloth poop to find the answers.

cooking the enemy

To a giant hornet, a beehive looks like an easy feast. Using its large yellow **mandibles**, the nearly two-inch-long hornet attacks the half-inch honeybees at lightning speed, crushing up to forty honeybees in one minute. And that's before it brings in **recruits**! Once a giant hornet scout finds a beehive, it marks the hive with a **chemical attractant** which acts like a sign that says, "Good eats here." The message draws dozens of other hornets to the nest, who join in a mass honeybee raid. A group of thirty hornets can destroy a colony of thirty thousand honeybees in just three hours. When they finish, the hornets carry the dead bees home to feed their young.

But Japanese honeybees have the perfect defense: they cook the enemy! Using their own bodies to do the job, hundreds of buzzing bees can create an enormous amount of "bee heat." That baking buzz is enough to turn an invading hornet into a crispy critter.

Creating heat is something that bees do all the time to warm their hive. They **shiver** (like people do when they're cold) by **contracting** or tightening their muscles, which produces lots of heat. Bees can contract their powerful wing muscles while holding very still, turning all their muscle energy into a hot defense mechanism.

Bees normally use their stingers to fight enemies, but that approach is useless against the thick, hard **exoskeleton** of a hornet. So, when a giant hornet attacks, the Japanese honeybees form a ball around the invader and begin to vibrate. Temperatures in the bee ball rise to a very hot 117°F; if you touched it, your skin would start to burn. Meanwhile, the honeybees can **tolerate** higher temperatures and are not bothered at all. The heated hornet, however, dies. Then, the bees push the unlucky intruder out of the nest and go about their business. With a combination of body heat and teamwork, the little bees destroy the giant enemy and save their hive.

1. Vietnamese bees use stinky poop to defend their hive from giant hornets. Worker bees gather bits of feces from buffalo, chickens, or pigs and carry it back to the hive in their mandibles. Then, they place small poop mounds around the outside of the hive entrance. While other bees don't seem to notice the smell, giant hornets are definitely put off. Once they sense the stink, the hornets fly in another direction, staying far, far away from the smelly hive.

2. Another special bee defense is to blast air from its anus. When small, pesky Argentine ants make their way to the entrance of a honeybee hive, worker bees point their rear ends at the invaders and rapidly fan their wings. The blast of air and a kick of the leg help to blow the ants right out of the nest.

making a toad puke its load

When an insect gets swallowed by a toad, it's usually done for. But a bombardier beetle has a crazy, wild way of freeing itself from the toad's stomach: it squirts poisonous hot juice from its rear end! A shot of that boiling liquid makes a toad puke up its prey, and the beetle races away unharmed.

How does the swallowed beetle survive in the toad's stomach in the first place? Its hard outer shell protects it from **digestive juices** . . . at least for a while. It takes around forty-five minutes for the insect to make its nasty juice, so if the beetle isn't fast enough, it will eventually get digested.

You may also wonder why the beetle isn't injured by its own poisonous brew. The bombardier carries the chemicals to make its poison in separate sacs inside its **abdomen**. When the bombardier is threatened by a predator, the muscles around these pouches contract to squeeze the chemicals into a third pouch. The ingredients combine into a new, explosive chemical that spews out of the beetle's rear end, right into the toad's mouth. This all happens so fast—in less than a second—that it doesn't hurt the beetle at all.

Being able to fill a predator's mouth with poison is a great defense, but a beetle can still get swallowed before it has a chance to spray. That's why a few species have developed this defense to spew their brew inside a predator's stomach.

There are over six hundred species of bombardiers living all over the world. They usually use their spray to keep predators such as frogs, toads, spiders, and ants far away. A beetle will point its rear directly at a predator and shoot the hot liquid onto the enemy's legs. They do this superfast, up to twenty times in a row, sending the predator running in the opposite direction. For a tiny insect that's less than one inch long (smaller than a quarter), these poison sprays are a powerful defense.

1. If getting vomited out isn't bad enough, imagine oozing out in poop! A small species of mud snail can survive for as long as five hours inside a duck's intestine and get pooped out alive. The hard shells and small size of these tiny snails keep them from getting digested quickly. Scientists believe that swallowed snails can get carried away or dispersed by the flying ducks to new islands or countries, where they crawl out of the poop and often start a whole new population.

2. A poisonous salamander called the rough-skinned newt is another animal that can escape from the inside of a frog. This red-bellied amphibian makes a toxin so poisonous that it kills its predator in minutes. Usually, when the newt sees danger, it displays its red belly, a warning that says, "I'm poisonous!" Seeing the red is enough to make most predators move on, but if a frog misses the warning and eats the toxic newt, the poisons in the prey's skin rapidly go to work. The frog becomes paralyzed and dies, while the newt escapes with no harm done.

23

a mouthful of froglets

When a Darwin's frog father gulps down his young, he's not eating them—he's protecting them! This thumb-sized dad stashes fifteen or more wiggling eggs or newly hatched **tadpoles** in his **vocal sacs**, the stretchy throat pouches that frogs use to make croaking sounds. The tadpoles remain hidden and protected for around two months as they mature into tiny froglets. Meanwhile, the amazing dad swells up like a tiny green balloon with a squirming mass inside.

Darwin's frogs are naturally found buried in **leaf litter** in the cool forests and streambeds of Chile and Argentina. With greenish-brown skin, tiny round bodies, and pointy snouts, these little frogs are well camouflaged, blending right into the leaf pile. Even when they are swollen with tadpoles, Darwin's frogs are hard for predators like snakes and birds to spot. Sitting very still, the fat frogs look more like a leaf than a tasty lunch.

Before he gulps up his kids, a Darwin's frog needs to find a ready mate. A female frog can lay up to twenty eggs on a wet patch of ground while the male **fertilizes** them with his **sperm**.

As soon as that's done, the mom is out of there, but the dad sticks around. He watches over his developing eggs for around two weeks. When the eggs start to wiggle, that means tadpoles are growing inside, and it's time to act! The dad gulps the eggs (or newly hatched tadpoles) down and pushes them under his tongue into his vocal sacs.

After seventy days, the tadpoles have metamorphosed into tiny, half-inch froglets. With a few coughs, the dad spews out a bunch of itsy-bitsy, tailless frogs. Amazing Dad has done his job, and the froglets are off and hopping through the leaves.

A peek at the tadpoles hidden inside the Darwin's frog father's vocal sacs.

1. Darwin's frogs aren't the only fathers that carry their eggs—there are fish that do it too. The hardhead catfish father carries up to forty-eight eggs in his mouth and goes without eating for two months while his young develop. That's a really devoted dad!

2. Central American **marsupial** frog mothers are likely to have lumps all over their backs, which can contain over 130 frog eggs! These eggs are packed into a pouch on a mother's back, where they safely develop into frogs. In one species, the horned marsupial frog, the eggs are fertilized by a male, who uses his hind feet to push the fertilized eggs into an opening in the mother's pouch. The eggs remain in their very swollen mom for as long as four months. When they are ready to emerge as tadpoles, their mom enters the water and uses her hind legs to squeeze them out.

oops, it's only a tail!

Ahungry snake lunges for a green iguana and ends up with . . . a tail! The lizard has run to safety, leaving its appendage behind. Meanwhile, the detached tail wiggles and jumps around for as long as a half an hour, totally confusing the snake.

Snapping off a body part sounds awful, but for most lizards it's a lifesaver. Even if a snake injects poison into its prey's tail, the lizard can pop it off in seconds, before the poison spreads.

So, how does the little reptile do it? The lizard's tail is designed with special cracks that can easily break with a squeeze of the muscles.

Losing a tail can create some problems—after all, a tail is a very helpful thing to have! It helps lizards balance when they run or jump or climb a tree. Without a tail, a lizard is much slower. Plus, lizards of the opposite sex aren't as interested in tailless partners. So, lizards don't give their tails up easily. A predator needs to pull hard or cut into the tail before it breaks off.

The good news is that most lizards can grow a new tail, although it can take some time, usually more than sixty days. The tail that grows back may

1. Some lizards not only pop off their own tails—they eat them! After a little brown skink has escaped from a predator, it often returns to the spot where the tail was dropped. The tail is where lizards store extra fat, making them highly nutritious. So, if the tail is still up for grabs, the skink eats it right up.

2. This snapping off of a body part, called autotomy, is used by many animals to escape predators. When a heron or other predator grabs a male fiddler crab's claw, the claw pops off, giving the crab time to skitter away. The crab has survived, but a one-clawed male can have trouble finding a mate or defending its sandy burrow from rivals. Still, losing a claw is a small sacrifice for staying alive.

3. Other animals that use autotomy to survive include spiders that will snap off a leg or two, starfish that can lose and replace an arm, and earthworms that lose a few parts of their heads or tails (but not too many) and make perfectly good replacement parts.

be a different color, and it will have bendable rods of **cartilage** instead of hard bone inside.

It's great that these tails grow back, but some lizards can end up with too much of a good thing—instead of one tail, they may grow two, three, or more! One lizard in Argentina was discovered with six tails coming off its rear end. That's a lot of tails!

27

frogcicles

Their hearts stop, their blood turns to ice, and they don't breathe . . . yet they're alive! Alaskan wood frogs survive supercold winters by turning into frogcicles. Living in the northern parts of Alaska and Canada, these one- to three-inch-long frogs are small enough to sit in the palm of your hand. Pick one up in the winter, though, and it will feel like an ice cube.

Becoming a block of ice can be a great way to stay alive when temperatures drop to 5°F. That's way below **freezing** (32°F, the temperature where water turns to ice). In order to make it through such cold winters, these small amphibians burrow under leaves or snow and stop almost everything: they don't eat, they don't drink, and they don't kick their legs. The only parts that don't freeze are the tiny **cells** that form their stomachs, livers, and other essential organs. These cells keep from freezing by filling with molecules of sugar (**glucose**) and a chemical in urine called **urea**. Glucose and urea work as **antifreezes**, chemicals that prevent water in the frog's cells from turning into ice. This keeps the cells from dying.

As temperatures rise in the spring, the wood frogs come back to life. They quickly start to warm up, or **thaw**. In just a few hours, their hearts start to beat.

Soon after, their blood flows, and they breathe again. Getting the legs fully kicking takes a bit longer— it can take up to two or three days before their muscles are fully warmed. After that, the wood frogs are hopping about, snatching insects with their long, sticky tongues. They'll continue to eat, mate, and lay eggs through the spring, summer, and fall. But as soon as the cold returns, these fascinating frogs will burrow down and turn back into frogcicles.

1. Black bears use their own urine to keep their muscles healthy when they hibernate, or sleep through the winter! While they don't let their bodies freeze like bats, ground squirrels, or other hibernators do, bears do slow down—they don't eat, drink, urinate, or defecate, living instead off stored body fat. Normally, when muscles aren't used, they start to shrink, but black bears have a way of stopping this—they reabsorb, or take back, their urine into their blood, using the urea in their liquid waste to rebuild their muscles. Urea can be broken down and rearranged to make muscle proteins, so when a bear wakes from hibernation, its muscles are ready for action.

2. Turning into a dried-out husk is another way to survive freezing temperatures. Arctic springtails, or snow fleas, survive Arctic winters by shriveling up and becoming inactive, losing nearly all of their water right through their cells. If the fleas don't have water, they can't freeze! They also make a special antifreeze, trehalose, that protects the little bit of remaining water inside them. As the ground begins to warm, springtails quickly sop up the melting soil water around them and become bouncy again.

tongues so blue the sun won't get through

A giraffe's tongue is a very dark, purply blue. At least, most of it is—in the very back of its throat, a giraffe's tongue is pink like those of most mammals. So why all the blue? It might be because giraffe tongues are always out in the sun! Scientists think that the blue color works like sunscreen, blocking the sun's **ultraviolet rays** and protecting against sunburn. Each day, giraffes use their tongues for sixteen to twenty hours to eat around seventy-five pounds of leaves. In the sunny African **savannah**, where giraffes live, it makes sense that those tongues would have good protection from the sun.

Those blue tongues are also amazing tools. They can stretch out to eighteen to twenty inches—about six times longer than our own three-inch tongues. They are also **prehensile**, like human thumbs, meaning they're able to twist and turn in almost every direction. Imagine if we could pick peas from a plate one by one with just our tongues. Not easy for us, but giraffes have it licked. Their long tongues can easily pick up small objects. They use their sunproof tongues to extend way back through the branches of spiky acacia trees and delicately pluck young leaves without getting pricked. So those extra-long, extra-twisty tongues aren't just blue—they're amazing tools as well.

1. Green blood? Wild! But not for green skink lizards—these insect-eating reptiles not only bleed green blood, but they also have green tongues, green bones, green skin, and tiny green hearts! The green comes from a pigment called biliverdin, which is a product of the chemical hemoglobin, which carries oxygen in red blood cells. The biliverdin seeps into the lizard's skin and bones and muscles, turning everything green. Humans also produce biliverdin. While it doesn't hurt the lizards, having too much of the green chemical is dangerous for humans, so our bodies quickly break it down—that's why people aren't green all over!

2. Green's not the only odd color of blood: tarantulas bleed blue! So do other spiders, crabs, snails, and octopuses. These blue bleeders have copper in their red blood cells, a chemical that turns blue when it's bonded (or attached) to oxygen. Another colorful bleeder is the leech—these little bloodsuckers bleed purple. There are even creatures whose blood has no color—the icefish of Antarctica has clear blood!

a whole deer for lunch

When a python swallows a deer, it gulps down the whole thing, hooves and all. That's over two hundred pounds of meat that the snake has to digest, or break down, really fast! Otherwise, that meal would rot inside the serpent's belly. So how do these slithery reptiles get it done? They grow new cells for their organs at superspeed—within hours after a python swallows a giant meal, its stomach, liver, and intestines start to expand. After just one day, these organs are nearly two times their normal size! The organ walls get extra thick and pour out digestive juices to break down every part of the prey—even skin and bones. The snake's heart gets bigger too. That way, after the python has finished digesting, it can easily move all the nutrients around its body through its blood. In just three days, most of the meal has turned to mush. In six days, only a ball of hair is left behind.

It all begins when the python's special **heat detectors** sense nearby prey. The large snake coils, springs, then sinks its sharp teeth into the victim, quickly wrapping itself around the deer and squeezing until its victim stops moving. Now it's time to swallow the enormous meal.

You may wonder how the python even gets its mouth around such large prey. At twenty feet long, a python is one enormous snake, but its mouth doesn't look big enough to swallow all that food at once. The trick is that the python has lots of **joints** between its jawbones. Human jaws have just one joint that moves like a hinge between the upper and lower jawbones, but a python's mouth has eight places where its jawbones come together. All these joints allow the python to open its mouth extra wide to take in a deer that is four times as wide as the snake's head. In addition, the python's lower jaw, or mandible, is made up of two separate bones (ours is just one) with a stretchy **ligament** holding them together. Helped along by the strong grip of the snake's long, sharp, backward-pointing teeth, the lower jawbones can move separately, pushing the deer down the throat.

By the end of one week, the python is done digesting, and its organs shrink back to their normal size. The snake doesn't need to waste energy by sending fuel to a big gut that's empty. Now, the well-fed python can just lie and wait for weeks or even months until the next big meal comes along.

A shrew saves energy by shrinking its head and brain! This mouse-sized mammal makes its home underground, passing the winter in an inactive, or torpid, state. Since shrews don't eat during this time, their organs shrink to conserve energy. Then in the spring, the brain and skull grow right back to their normal size and the shrew can skitter off in search of insects and seeds to munch.

up a hummingbird's nose and off it goes

Hitching a ride in a hummingbird's nose is the perfect way to fly—that is, if you're an itsy-bitsy mite! Hummingbird flower mites are tiny spider relatives that must move between flowers to find mates and to drink enough flower **nectar**. The flower mites are just one of the over fifty thousand species of mites that live in soil, water, or inside and outside of larger animals. Since flower mites are only the size of a pencil tip and wingless, their eight tiny legs don't get them very far. The fastest way to travel, it turns out, is up a hummingbird's nose.

When a flower runs out of nectar, the mites get ready to leave their food source. As soon as a hummingbird pokes its beak into their flower, the mites hop on board. The hummingbirds don't stay for long, so the little mites must be superquick—in seconds, they dash onto the hummingbird's beak and crawl up into the bird's nostrils. Here they join as many as fifteen fellow mites hanging on tight as the hummingbird zips through the air.

Once the hummingbird lands on a new flower, the mites must decide if it's the right kind. There are lots of different species of flower mites (at least fifty have been found so far), and each likes its own kind of flower. If the tiny traveler gets it wrong, it risks getting chased or killed by mites of other species. Plus, mites are looking for more than food—they also seek mates, and they need to land on the right flower to find them. So, they must decide quickly, before their ride moves on. They investigate with tiny chemical-sensing hairs on their legs called **setae**, which can detect the scent of the right nectar from the right flower.

Inside the perfect flower, the hummingbird mites suck up nectar, mate, and lay eggs. Newly hatched larval mites may live out their two-week life right where they hatched, but if the flower's nectar runs low or they need to find a mate, it's time to move. That's when they hitch a ride on a hummingbird "plane."

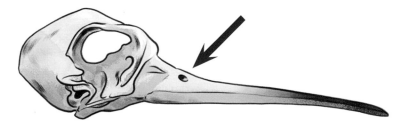

A hummingbird's skull showing the nasal opening where the mites crawl in.

1. Nearly every kind of animal has one or more species of mite living in or on it—even humans! Dust mites feed on dead skin cells, and since humans normally flake off or lose millions of dead skin cells every day, there's plenty of food in our homes for these tiny critters. Some people are allergic to mite feces (or poop) and end up with coughs, drippy noses, and itchy eyes and skin. But since these guys are microscopic and don't bite, we don't normally notice the millions and millions living all around us.

2. The inside of a honeybee is an ideal home for one species of mite. Tracheal mites spend most of their lives inside a bee's trachea, or breathing tube. The mites hatch out of eggs and grow into adults in about twenty days, all inside the bee. Then, the mites use their sharp mouthparts to pierce the bee's trachea and suck out its bloodlike body fluid called hemolymph. Mature tracheal mites usually stay inside the bee, but female mites often leave an old bee to find a younger, healthier host and new mites to mate with. Infected bees have deformed wings and may not live through their normal one- to three-month lives. An arrangement like this one where one animal benefits (the mite) and the other is harmed (the bee) is called parasitism.

ant shampoo

Ant shampoo—doesn't sound very appealing, right? Well, it's perfect for birds that have lice and mites burrowing into their skin. With only their beaks to pick away at nasty invaders, many birds rely on ant baths to speed up the process. An itchy robin often plops right on top of an anthill, pressing its wings and body into the crawling mass of insects. Alarmed ants quickly stream all over the bird, spewing **formic acid** from their rear ends. The formic acid doesn't bother the ant but kills other small critters, working as a **pesticide** that helps the ant fight off predators. The acid seems to help birds fight pesky parasites as well. An "anting" robin uses its beak to help spread the ants around to extra itchy spots. The whole process of ant bathing can take minutes or up to an hour.

Some birds like blue jays prefer a one-ant-at-a-time approach. The jay crushes an ant in its bill, squeezing out the formic acid. Then it smears the squished insect over any itchy body parts. Never one to waste good food, the blue jay often gobbles down a used-up ant before finding another to squish.

Bathing with ants must really work, because

1. If rubbing ants on your skin sounds bad, imagine rubbing millipedes on your rear end! Madagascar lemurs (primates that are distantly related to monkeys) use a millipede's toxic juices on their rear ends, or anuses, to fight off nasty threadworms that can live in their digestive tracts. The millipedes, which are insectlike critters with hundreds of legs, make **hydrochloric acid** and other poisons to fight off predators. Lemurs capture and chew the squiggly critters and rub them all around their anuses. The threadworms leave the lemur's anus at night to lay eggs in the surrounding skin, but the millipede juices will kill the worms. After a thorough chewing and rubbing, some of the lemurs then swallow the millipedes, legs and all!

2. The Florida carpenter ant is one of several species that uses its own poisonous formic acid to keep its insides clean. It turns out that the toxic chemical is not just useful for fighting predators; it can also kill microbes in the ant's gut. So when these ants spew out acid, they rub their mouthparts on their rear ends, picking up drops of the liquid with their food. The acid fights off most bacteria that would otherwise invade the insects' digestive tracts. We humans also have hydrochloric acid in our stomachs that helps with digestion and fights bacteria that come in our food. This acid is made by special glands in the stomach wall, so we don't have to eat it like carpenter ants do.

lots of different species of birds do it. Anters include crows, ravens, owls, turkeys, pheasants, sparrows, and many others. In fact, over two hundred different species of birds have been observed taking ant baths. And if ants aren't nearby, other critters may be used, like caterpillars, grasshoppers, snails, and even wasps!

a rat catastrophe

Cat pee—oh no! If you're a rat, you know you'd better run; otherwise, you could easily become dinner. But if you're a rat infected with a parasite called *Toxoplasma gondii*, you'll get it all wrong and run right into the cat's waiting paws. For some unlucky rodents, toxoplasma changes the brain, making a rat run toward a cat instead of away from it.

So how do rats get this nasty invader? It all starts with cat feces (poop). Rats are **omnivores**, meaning they eat almost anything, including rotten fruits and vegetables, dead animals, and cat feces. But when that feces is loaded with toxoplasma, that means trouble for the rat. As soon as the microscopic parasite gets swallowed, it moves into the blood and goes straight to the rat's brain. There, it releases chemicals that turn off the rat's **fear center**. The infected rat is not afraid of the smell of cat urine (pee), so it runs toward the cat instead of away. Then, *snap*, the cat catches the rat.

Toxoplasma needs to grow inside both cats and rats to complete its **life cycle**. For the parasite to survive, a rat has to eat infected cat poop, and then a cat has to eat that infected rat. So, the toxoplasma has **evolved** amazing ways to make this happen by getting into and changing the rat's brain.

Once the cat eats the rat, the toxoplasmas are where they need to be: inside the cat's intestine. Here the parasites reproduce, making millions of new parasites. The young parasites are small round balls, called **oocysts**. Oocysts can only finish their growth and mature inside a rat. That process starts when the cat poops out millions of oocysts. Rats get a big mouthful of the parasites when they gobble up cat feces, which starts the whole life cycle all over again.

After an infected cat poops, the rat eats the parasite-filled poop. The infected rat runs toward the cat and is easy to catch.

1. A grasshopper won't normally go near water, but when a hairworm burrows into the insect's brain, everything changes. When a grasshopper accidently eats grass with hairworm larvae on it, the long, skinny hairworms move into the grasshopper's intestine and live off the nutrients inside. The hairworms grow as much as six inches, filling the grasshopper's body. Then it's time for the hairworms to find a mate. By releasing brain-altering chemicals, the parasites change the grasshopper into a water seeker. Instead of avoiding a nearby pond, the grasshopper jumps right in! The grasshopper dies, and the hairworm quickly wiggles out and swims off to find a mate.

2. The ichneumonid wasp makes a spider its servant. The spider normally weaves orb webs to catch prey, but when a female wasp lays an egg on the spider's back, everything changes. The wasp larva hatches and lives off the spider, feeding on the spider's insides. After around fourteen days, the larva releases chemicals that make the spider build a special cocoon support web. Then the larva kills and eats the spider, building a cocoon on the web. Here, the larva will mature into an adult, fly off to look for a mate, and eventually find another spider to reprogram.

glossary

Abdomen: The cavity or space in the body under the rib cage, below the large, flat breathing muscle called the diaphragm. The abdomen contains many organs, including the stomach, liver, pancreas, small intestine, large intestine, kidneys, spleen, and urinary bladder.

Algae: A simple, nonflowering, and typically aquatic plant that contains chlorophyll but lacks true stems, roots, leaves, and vascular tissue.

Amphibians: A group of animals that includes frogs, toads, and salamanders. Amphibians are vertebrates, meaning they have backbones, and they do not have scales on their skin. They live both on the land and in the water.

Antifreezes: Chemicals that keep liquids from forming ice. They may be salts, sugars, proteins, or other chemicals that prevent water molecules from binding or attaching to one another.

Anus: The opening at the lowest part of an animal's digestive tract and a part of the large intestine known as the anal canal. Undigested foods leave an animal's body by passing through the anus as waste.

Apes: Large primates, including chimpanzees, gorillas, orangutans, and gibbons, that do not have tails. They are found in Asia and Africa.

Autotomy: The popping-off of a tail or leg by animals like salamanders, crabs, and spiders as a way of escaping from a predator. The lost limb or tail usually grows back after a period of months.

Barb: The sharp, pointed part of something like an arrow or fishhook. The barbed end of a woodpecker's tongue allows it to pierce and snatch insects from inside a tree hole.

Biliverdin: A compound formed when red hemoglobin from blood gets broken down in the body. Biliverdin is green. These chemicals add color to urine, feces, and bruises.

Bond: A connection between chemicals. Molecules like proteins, fats, and carbohydrates are made up of smaller molecules, which are held together by bonds.

Bull: The term used for some adult male animals, such as cows, elephants, whales, and seals.

Camouflage: The way animals hide from predators or prey by having the same colors or shapes of their surroundings.

Cartilage: A bonelike tissue that gives support and shape to some parts of the body but is not as hard as bone. It is found in the ears and nose, and as a smooth protective cover on the ends of bones.

Cells: The basic building block units of all living things. Every part of the body is made up of cells. There are many different kinds of cells in the body, each with its own function.

Chemical attractant: A chemical produced by one animal that draws in or attracts other animals of a species for mating or for sending a message that food is nearby.

Cocoon: A covering made of silky threads that the larvae of moths, butterflies, and some other insects form around themselves. Inside the cocoon, the larvae are protected as they mature into an adult form.

Contracting: When the fibers inside a muscle move together to do work, the muscle is contracting. This means they produce something called force, a power that can be used to hold up parts of the body like the head, move body parts like the arms and legs, or move things inside the body like the stomach and intestines.

Copper: A metal that is found in the blood cells of some animals, like spiders, snails, and crabs. When it is bonded (or chemically attached) to oxygen, it turns blue and gives these animals blue blood.

Defecate: The release of feces or digestive wastes from the body through the large intestine.

Digest: The breaking down of an object into smaller parts. Food that is broken down has been digested. Animals digest food to get useful nutrients from it.

Digestive juices: Chemicals made by organs like the stomach and intestines that help to break down or digest food.

Digestive tract: The series of organs that food passes through when eaten. These organs include the mouth, esophagus, stomach, small intestine, and large intestine.

Dipole field: The circle of electricity that an electric fish creates around itself to detect changes that objects make to the shape of the circle.

Dispersed: The spreading out of something over a large area. If you blow on the seeds of a dandelion, you disperse, or send, its seeds out into the air.

Dung: A term used for feces or digestive wastes that are defected or released from the large intestine.

Electric organs: An organ made up of specialized muscle or nerve cells used by electric fish to produce an electric discharge or field outside of its body.

Electric pulses: Waves of electricity released from electric organs or nerve or muscle cells.

Electroreceptors: Specialized sensors found in water-dwelling animals, such as sharks, rays, and electric fish like eels and elephantnose fish, that allow them to detect electricity from other animals. These small electricity detectors are often scattered over the face and sides of the animal.

Estrous: The periods of time when a female mammal is ready to mate and will accept a male. During this time, the female is described as being in heat.

Evolve: To change gradually. Animal species can evolve or change over many, many years so that they can live in or move into different or changing environments.

Exoskeleton: The hard outer covering that supports or holds up and protects an animal's body, such as the outer coverings of beetles and the shells of lobsters, crabs, and turtles.

Fart: A small explosion of gas coming from the large intestine. Depending on the amount and type of gases inside, farts may also be noisy and stinky.

Fear center: A part of the brain where animals feel fear in response to a scary situation.

Feces: Wastes formed in the large intestine from the parts of food left behind after digestion.

Fertilize: Fertilization occurs when the sperm from a male animal comes together with the egg from a female animal.

Formic acid: A stinging chemical that is made by some ants and sprayed on predators and prey.

Freezing: The cold temperature at which a liquid turns into a solid. When water freezes at 32°F, it turns into ice.

Frequencies: The frequency of a sound wave is the rate at which (or how quickly) a sound wave vibrates in the air. A fast-frequency sound wave is high-pitched and sounds screechy, while a slow-frequency sound wave is lower pitched and sounds deeper.

Global warming: The slow warming of the Earth's surface, atmosphere, and oceans. Scientists believe that one cause of global warming is high levels of greenhouse gases, like carbon dioxide—which forms when we burn fuel like coal, oil, and gasoline—and methane from cows.

Glucose: A kind of sugar. It is one of the main chemicals broken down by cells for energy.

Greenhouse effect: Gases in our atmosphere trap heat. By keeping heat close to the earth, these gases are thought to contribute to global warming.

Heat detectors: Some snakes have special sense organs (or pit organs) that detect heat coming from the bodies of other animals. Pit organs, which are located on the faces of pythons, boas, and other snakes, allow the predators to "see" a heat image of warm prey in the dark.

Hemoglobin: A chemical in our red blood cells that carries oxygen from the lungs throughout the body.

Hemolymph: A bloodlike liquid that moves around the bodies of invertebrates (animals without backbones), like insects and crabs. Like blood, hemolymph carries nutrients to different organs and transports waste away from them. Unlike blood, hemolymph is not carried in blood vessels, but instead goes directly to all the parts of the animal.

Hibernate, Hibernation: When an animal hibernates, it withdraws from the outside world and slows down its breathing, heart rate, and digestion.

Host: A living animal or plant that has another organism living on or inside its body. The guest may get food, shelter, and protection from its host.

Hydrochloric acid: A strong acid that is produced in the stomachs of most animals and helps to break down food during digestion.

Infect: When one organism lives in or on another host organism, scientists say that the host organism is infected.

Intestine: The lower part of the digestive tract in vertebrates (animals with backbones). It is made up of two organs: the small intestine, which is a long, skinny passageway where food is digested, and the large intestine, a fatter passageway where wastes are formed and eliminated from the body as feces.

Joints: The places where two bones come together. The bones in a joint are held together by strong tissues.

Lamella: Very thin, flat structures of bone or other tough tissues that enable some animals to stick to things.

Larvae: Young animals that will mature and change into different adult forms. This change is known as metamorphosis.

Leaf litter: A pile of leaves, twigs, and bark that has fallen from the trees to the ground. The pile creates an excellent hiding place for many animals and insects.

Life cycle: The series of changes that take place in a plant or animal or other organism during its stages of life.

Ligament: A tough band of tissue that holds bones together.

Mammals: Vertebrates (animals with backbones) that feed their young with milk and have hair on their bodies. They are also endothermic, meaning their bodies are able to keep their temperature at the same level even when the surrounding temperatures change.

Mandible: The mouthparts or jaws of many animals. In snakes, humans, and others, the mandible is the lower, moveable jawbone.

Marsupial: A mammal whose young are born at a very early stage in development. The young, which are tiny and immature, complete their development in their mother's pouch or skinfold.

Metamorphose: When animals metamorphose, they go through several steps to change from an embryo to an adult (see also life cycle).

Methane: A gas released into the air by burning fuel, burping cows, and the bacterial breakdown of garbage. Methane traps heat in the air and plays an important part in warming the earth (see also global warming).

Microbes: Living organisms that are so small, humans can only see them with a microscope. Microbes include organisms like bacteria and viruses (although not all scientists agree that viruses are living things).

Microscopic: Something that is microscopic is so small that you can only see it with a microscope.

Mucus lining: A layer of mucus that coats the insides of organ passages that open to the outside. This includes an animal's digestive tracts, respiratory tracts, and urinary tracts. The mucus protects the organ walls by trapping dirt and microbes.

Musth: A condition in bull, or adult male, elephants that occurs once a year when they are ready to mate. The period of musth lasts for two to three months.

Mutualism: A link between two organisms in which both benefit from being together.

Nectar: A sugary liquid made by plants to attract animals.

Nostril: One of two holes that open into the nose.

Nutrients: The sugars, fats, proteins, and vitamins in food.

Omnivores: Animals that eat both plants and animals.

Oocysts: A stage of development for tiny parasites called protozoa that infect other living things. The oocyst contains a fertilized egg or zygote, covered by a protective shell, allowing them to remain safely inside a host animal's intestines or muscles.

Orb webs: These spiderwebs are shaped like wheels, with rings and lines (or spokes) running through them. Most are remade every day. Not all spiders are orb weavers—some species build messy cobwebs.

Ossicles: The very tiny bones inside the ears of vertebrates that pick up sound waves and amplify or magnify them and send or transmit them to the hearing receptors deep inside the ear.

Oxygen: A gas that is found in the air we breathe. It is picked up in our lungs by the hemoglobin in our blood, then carried to our bodies' cells and used to make energy.

Paralyzed: When an animal is paralyzed, it cannot move.

Parasites, Parasitism: Animals that live and feed on or in other living organisms and harm them in the process. The behavior of a parasite is called parasitism.

Pesticide: A toxic chemical that is used to kill or repel plants and animals that are considered pests.

Pheromones: Chemicals produced by an animal that change the behavior of other animals. Pheromones may be used to attract mates and warn other animals of danger.

Predators: Animals that get food by killing and eating other animals.

Prehensile: A part of the body that can curl around an object and grab it. Humans have prehensile thumbs.

Primates: A group or order of mammals that include monkeys, apes, humans, and lemurs. They grow nails on their hands and feet and have large brains.

Proboscis: A long, skinny tube that acts as the mouth for some insects, like butterflies.

Proteins: Large molecules that have many important roles in our bodies, including forming muscles, bones, and other tissues; forming enzymes, which speed chemical reactions; and forming hemoglobin, which carries oxygen in the blood.

Reabsorb: To take back something that has been released or put out.

Recruits: Extra animals that work with an animal that is hunting or fighting.

Red blood cells: Microscopic round cells found in blood, which carry oxygen from the lungs to all the tissues of the body.

Reprogram: To change how something works.

Reptiles: Vertebrates (animals with backbones) that have lungs, scales, and lay eggs. They regulate their body temperatures by sunning and burrowing in the ground. They include lizards, turtles, alligators, and snakes.

Respiratory tract: The pathway or tract that carries air to and from the lungs. The tract includes the mouth, nose, throat, and the trachea (a tube that runs from the throat to the lungs).

Savannah: A warm grassland that has scattered trees and shrubs.

School: A group of fish that swim together, turning and twisting at the same time. Schooling fish can confuse predators because they are hard to pick out from the pack.

Setae: Small stiff hairs found on the bodies of many animals, such as insects, worms, and mites. The tiny hairs can work as chemical sensors.

Shiver: When you shiver, your muscles

contract and relax quickly, causing shaking. Contracting muscles also make heat, so shivering warms the body.

Shriveling: Shrinking or getting smaller.

Slime: A thick, sticky liquid produced by some animals for protection and communication.

Species: A group of animals, plants, or other living organisms that are similar to one another and can mate with one another to produce young. Animals usually cannot mate with animals of other species.

Sperm: Male sex cells produced by animals and plants. When animals mate or plants are pollinated, the sperm unite with eggs from females to make a new organism.

Suction cup: A round object or part of the body that can be pressed down onto something and stuck to it.

Sugars: Chemicals that animals use for energy. Some sugars include glucose, fructose (fruit sugar), and lactose (milk sugar).

Swim bladder: A gas-filled pouch that many fish have inside their bodies. The fish fills the pouch to become more buoyant or float up in the water and empties the bladder to move down.

Symbiosis: An interaction between animals of two species in which both get something good out of it.

Synchronize: When things are synchronized with each other, they do the same thing at the same time.

Tadpoles: Young, newly hatched frogs and toads. They have tails and gills and breathe in the water. As they change or metamorphose into their adult forms,

tadpoles grow legs and lungs, and lose their tails and gills.

Tendons: Tough, thick tissues that attach muscles to the bones that they move.

Thaw: To melt or go from a frozen state to a liquid or soft state. When ice is warmed, it thaws and turns into water.

Tolerate: To be able to deal with a difficult situation.

Toxin: A chemical that is poisonous enough to injure or kill some plants or animals.

Trachea: The breathing tube in animals that carries air from the throat to the lungs.

Trehalose: A kind of sugar that some animals have in their blood that works like antifreeze to keep them from freezing in the winter.

Ultraviolet rays: Ultraviolet, or UV, radiation is a form of invisible energy from sunlight that penetrates skin. UV rays help humans and other animals make vitamin D, but too much can cause a dangerous sunburn.

Urea: A chemical waste found in urine. Some animals that live in supercold climates keep urea in their blood as an antifreeze to prevent their body fluids from freezing (see also **trehalose**).

Urine: A yellow, liquid waste (also called pee) that is formed in the kidneys and released from the urinary bladder. To urinate is to release urine from the body.

Vibrations: Very fast back and forth movements. Sound waves can cause vibrations in the air and in the ground.

Vocal sacs: Pouches in the mouths of frogs that swell up to make their calls louder.